MAKE MONEY BY DOING BLOGGING IN 2023 - BY TECH KIRAN

KIRAN KUMAR

Contents

CHAPTER ONE

What is Blogging?

Blogging is the practice of regularly creating and publishing content on the internet through a blog. A blog is a type of website that features written content, often organized into specific categories or topics, and is updated frequently with new posts.

Blogs can cover a wide range of topics, such as personal experiences, news, politics, technology, lifestyle, and many more. They are usually maintained by an individual or a small group of people, and often allow readers to leave comments on the posts.

Blogging has become a popular way for people to share their thoughts, ideas, and expertise with a wide audience, and can also be used as a platform for businesses to connect with their customers and promote their products or services.

Can I do blogging without any graduation?

Yes, you can start a blog without any graduation. A college degree is not a requirement for starting a blog, and many successful bloggers do not have formal education in writing or journalism. The most important thing is to have a passion for writing and a knowledge or interest in the topic you want to blog about.

Having good writing skills and the ability to create engaging content is important for making your blog successful. Blogging also requires some technical skills, such as setting up a website and understanding how to use social media to promote your blog. However, these skills can be learned through online tutorials, classes and practice.

In addition, it is not necessary to have a degree to start a blog, but it can help you in writing and understanding how to create a good content strategy, how to promote your blog and how to monetize it.

In summary, while a degree is not required to start a blog, it is important to have strong writing skills, knowledge of your topic, and the ability to learn the technical skills needed to create and maintain a successful blog.

CHAPTER TWO

How do I start Blogging?

Starting a blog is relatively easy and can be done in a few simple steps:

- **Choose a topic**: Decide on a specific topic or niche that you want to write about. This could be something you are passionate about or have expertise in.
- **Choose a blogging platform**: There are many free and paid blogging platforms available, such as WordPress, Blogger, and Squarespace. WordPress is the most popular and widely used platform, it offers a lot of customization options and it's easy to use.
- **Choose a web host**: A web host is a service that stores your blog on a server and makes it accessible to the internet. If you choose WordPress, you can use WordPress.com to host your blog for free or you can use a hosting service like Bluehost, Siteground, etc.
- **Design your blog**: Once you've chosen a platform and web host, you can customize the design and layout of your blog to make it look unique.
- **Start creating content**: Once your blog is set up, you can start creating and publishing content. Be consistent in

your posting schedule and try to publish new content on a regular basis.

- **Promote your blog**: Share your blog posts on social media and other platforms, and use SEO techniques to make your blog more visible in search engines.
- **Monetize your blog**: There are many ways to monetize your blog, such as through advertising, affiliate marketing, sponsored posts, and selling products or services.

It's important to keep in mind that starting a blog takes time and effort. But with consistent effort, patience, and a good content strategy, you can build a successful blog.

CHAPTER THREE

What is web hosting and which place is best for hosting my site?

Web hosting is a service that allows you to store your website files on a server, and make them accessible to the internet. When a user types in your website's address in their browser, the browser sends a request to the server where your website is hosted, and the server sends back the files that make up your website, which the browser then displays to the user.

There are many web hosting companies and services available, each with different features and pricing plans. Some popular options include:

- **Shared hosting**: This is the most basic and inexpensive option, where you share a server with other websites. It's suitable for small and personal websites or blogs.
- **VPS hosting**: This is a more advanced option, where you have your own virtual server. It's suitable for medium-sized websites or blogs that require more resources.

- **Dedicated hosting**: This is the most expensive option, where you have your own physical server. It's suitable for large and complex websites that require a lot of resources.
- **Cloud hosting**: This is a newer option, where you can scale your resources on demand and pay only for what you use. It's suitable for websites that experience a lot of traffic or need to handle large amounts of data.

When choosing a web hosting company, it's important to consider factors such as the uptime guarantee, the type of server, the security features, the customer support, the pricing, and the scalability options.

Some of the best web hosting providers are:

Bluehost

Siteground

A2 Hosting

HostGator

Dreamhost

It's always recommended to check reviews and compare the features, pricing and support of different hosting providers before making a decision. Some providers are specialized in certain types of websites and some are better for beginners, some are more expensive but offer more features and some are cheaper but have less support.

Keep in mind that choosing a web hosting provider depends on the needs and goals of your website, so it's important to evaluate your website's needs and choose a provider that fits those needs.

CHAPTER FOUR

Is WordPress the best platform?

WordPress is a popular and widely used content management system (CMS) that is often used as a platform for creating and managing websites, particularly blogs. It's considered one of the best platforms for blogging because it's free, open-source, and has a large and active community of users and developers.

Some of the features that make WordPress a great platform for blogging include:

- **Easy to use**: WordPress is user-friendly, with a simple and intuitive interface that makes it easy to create and manage content.
- **Customizable**: WordPress has a wide range of templates and plugins that can be used to customize the design and functionality of your website.
- **SEO friendly**: WordPress is optimized for search engines, and there are many plugins that can help you improve your website's visibility in search engines.
- **Scalable**: WordPress can be used for small personal blogs, as well as large and complex websites.

Additionally, WordPress is a self-hosted platform, which means you have full control over your website, and you can customize it to your needs. You can also add new features and functionalities with the use of plugins and themes.

However, it's also worth noting that WordPress does have some limitations and it might not be the best option for certain types of websites. For example, if you need a website with a lot of dynamic content or a lot of custom features, other platforms like Squarespace or Shopify might be a better fit.

In summary, WordPress is considered a best platform for blogging and it's a great choice for most websites, especially if you want a platform that is easy to use, customizable, SEO-friendly, and scalable. It's always good to check and compare the features and pricing of different platforms before making a decision.

What are the best themes for WordPress?

There are thousands of WordPress themes available, both free and paid, that can be used to customize the design and layout of your website. Some popular options include:

- **Astra**: A lightweight and customizable theme that is suitable for all types of websites. It offers a variety of design options and is optimized for performance.
- **Divi**: A highly customizable theme that allows you to create custom layouts and designs using a drag-and-drop interface. It's suitable for creating complex websites.
- **GeneratePress**: A lightweight and customizable theme that is suitable for all types of websites. It's optimized for performance and accessibility.
- **OceanWP**: A free and flexible theme that is suitable for all types of websites. It's optimized for performance and has a variety of design options.
- **Neve**: A lightweight and customizable theme that is suitable for all types of websites. It's optimized for

performance and has a variety of design options.

- **Avada**: A highly customizable theme that is suitable for creating complex websites. It has a lot of design options and a drag-and-drop interface.
- **StudioPress Themes**: A collection of high-quality and customizable themes that are suitable for all types of websites. They are built on the Genesis framework, which is optimized for performance and security.
- **Hestia**: A free and customizable theme that is suitable for all types of websites. It's optimized for performance and has a variety of design options.

It's important to note that the best theme for your website will depend on your specific needs and goals. Some themes are better suited for specific types of websites, such as e-commerce, portfolios, blogs, etc. It's always recommended to preview the themes and check the features and the reviews before installing.

It's also worth noting that the theme is just one aspect of your website and it's not the only thing that makes a website good. A good content, user-friendly interface, responsive design, and good performance are also important factors for a good website.

CHAPTER SIX

How to write best content in blogging?

Writing good content for your blog is essential for attracting and retaining readers. Here are some tips for writing great blog content:

- **Research your topic**: Make sure you understand the topic you're writing about, and gather information from reliable sources.
- **Be unique and original**: Avoid copying content from other sources, and try to add your own perspective and insights to the topic.
- **Write in a conversational tone**: Use a tone that is easy to understand and engaging for your readers.
- **Use headings, bullet points, and images**: Make your content visually appealing and easy to skim by using headings, bullet points, and images.
- **Keep it concise and to the point**: Avoid rambling and stick to the main points of your topic.
- **Use keywords**: Use relevant keywords in your content to help it rank well in search engines.
- **Use internal and external links**: Link to other relevant content on your blog, as well as to external sources that

provide additional information on your topic.

- **Proofread and edit**: Make sure your content is free of errors, grammatical mistakes and punctuation mistakes.
- **Promote your content**: Share your content on social media and other platforms, and use SEO techniques to make your blog more visible in search engines.
- **Be consistent**: Be consistent in your posting schedule and try to publish new content on a regular basis.

Writing great content takes time and effort, but by following these tips, you can create content that is informative, engaging, and appealing to your readers. Remember that your audience is the most important part of your blog, so always keep them in mind when creating your content.

CHAPTER SEVEN

What is SEO?

SEO stands for Search Engine Optimization, it is the practice of optimizing a website to improve its ranking in search engine results pages (SERPs) and increase the quantity and quality of its organic traffic.

Search engines like Google, Bing, or Yahoo use complex algorithms to determine the relevance and authority of a website and its pages and to match a user's search query to the most relevant and useful results. SEO techniques aim to make a website more attractive to search engines by making it more relevant, useful, and trustworthy.

SEO can be divided into two main categories: On-page SEO and Off-page SEO.

On-page SEO refers to the optimization of the website's content and HTML source code, and it includes the following elements:

Title tags
Headings
Meta descriptions
URL structure
Content quality
Keyword research
Images and videos optimization

Off-page SEO refers to the optimization of external factors that affect the website's authority and visibility, and it includes the following elements:

Backlinks

Social media signals

Brand mentions

Online reviews

SEO is a continuous process and it's important to keep track of the search engine's updates and changes. Additionally, SEO is not a one-time process, it requires a consistent effort and it might take some time to see the results.

It's also important to note that SEO is not just about ranking higher in the SERPs, it's also about providing a better user experience and making a website more useful, relevant and trustworthy.

CHAPTER EIGHT

What is technical SEO?

Technical SEO is the process of optimizing a website's technical infrastructure, including the HTML source code, the website structure, and the server environment to improve its visibility and ranking in search engine results pages (SERPs). It involves making sure that a website is properly indexed by search engines and that it is easily accessible and usable for both search engine crawlers and users.

Technical SEO includes the following elements:

- **Site structure and navigation**: A well-organized site structure with clear navigation makes it easier for search engines to crawl and index your site, and for users to find the content they are looking for.
- **URL structure**: A clear and consistent URL structure makes it easy for search engines to understand the hierarchy of your website and the relationship between different pages.
- **Robots.txt file**: This file tells search engines which pages or sections of your site they should not crawl, and it's important to use it properly so the search engines

can focus on the important pages of your site.

- **XML Sitemaps**: An XML sitemap is a file that lists all the URLs of your site and helps search engines to find and crawl all the pages of your site.
- **Canonicalization**: This is the process of specifying the preferred version of a web page, it's important to avoid duplicate content issues.
- **Redirects**: Redirects are used to redirect users and search engines from an old or broken URL to a new one, it's important to use the proper type of redirects to avoid any issues.
- **Website speed**: A fast loading website improves the user experience, and it's also a ranking factor for search engines.
- **Mobile-friendliness**: A mobile-friendly website is important for the user experience, and it's also a ranking factor for search engines.
- **Security**: A secure website (HTTPS) is important for the user experience, and it's also a ranking factor for search engines.

Technical SEO is a crucial aspect of SEO and it's important to pay attention to it, as it lays the foundation for a website's visibility and ranking in search engines. Additionally, it's important to keep track of the search engine's updates and changes and make sure that your website is up-to-date.

CHAPTER NINE

What is off-page SEO?

Off-page SEO refers to the optimization of external factors that affect the visibility and ranking of a website in search engine results pages (SERPs). It involves promoting a website through external sources and building its authority, credibility and trustworthiness.

Off-page SEO includes the following elements:

- **Backlinks**: Backlinks are links from other websites to your website, they are considered a vote of confidence in your site's content and they also help to improve the visibility and ranking of your site.
- **Social media signals**: Social media shares, likes and followers are considered a sign of engagement and popularity and can help to boost a website's visibility and ranking.
- **Brand mentions**: Mentioning a brand or website without linking to it is also considered a sign of popularity and relevance, and it can help to boost a website's visibility and ranking.
- **Online reviews**: Positive reviews on sites like Yelp, TripAdvisor, etc. can help to boost a website's visibility and reputation.

- **Directories**: Being listed in directories like Yelp, TripAdvisor, etc. can also help to boost a website's visibility and reputation.
- **Influencer marketing**: Partnering with influencers can help to promote a website and build its reputation.

Off-page SEO is a continuous process that requires a consistent effort, it can take some time to see the results, but it's important to keep track of the progress and make sure that the external sources are reputable and relevant. Additionally, it's important to keep in mind that off-page SEO is not only about getting backlinks, it's also about building a website's reputation and authority.

CHAPTER TEN

What is on-page SEO?

On-page SEO refers to the optimization of a website's content and HTML source code to improve its visibility and ranking in search engine results pages (SERPs). It involves making sure that a website is properly indexed by search engines and that it is easily accessible and usable for both search engine crawlers and users.

On-page SEO includes the following elements:

- **Title tags**: Title tags are the text that appears in the browser tab, they are used by search engines to understand the content of a page, and they should be unique and descriptive.
- **Headings**: Headings (H1, H2, H3, etc.) are used to organize the content of a page and they should be used to indicate the hierarchy of the content.
- **Meta descriptions**: Meta descriptions are short summaries of a page's content, they appear in the SERPs and they should be unique and descriptive.
- **URL structure**: A clear and consistent URL structure makes it easy for search engines to understand the hierarchy of your website and the relationship between different pages.

- **Content quality**: The content of a page should be unique, relevant and useful, it should also be well-written and free of spelling and grammar errors.
- **Keyword research**: Identifying the relevant keywords for a page's content and including them in the title tags, headings, and content can help to boost the visibility and ranking of a page.

CHAPTER ELEVEN

What are the best plugins for WordPress site?

There are thousands of WordPress plugins available, both free and paid, that can be used to add new features and functionality to your website. Some popular options include:

- **Yoast SEO**: This plugin helps to optimize your website for search engines by providing tools for keyword research, creating XML sitemaps, and analyzing the content of your pages.
- **Akismet**: This plugin helps to protect your website from spam comments by checking all comments against a global database of spam.
- **Jetpack**: This plugin provides a variety of features such as security, performance optimization, and analytics.
- **W3 Total Cache**: This plugin helps to improve the performance of your website by caching and minifying your pages and posts.

- **Gravity Forms**: This plugin allows you to create and manage forms on your website, such as contact forms, surveys and polls.
- **WPForms**: A popular plugin that allows you to create and manage forms on your website, it's user-friendly and it has a drag-and-drop interface.
- **Yoast SEO**: A popular plugin that helps to optimize your website for search engines by providing tools for keyword research, creating XML sitemaps, and analyzing the content of your pages.
- **WP Smush**: This plugin helps to optimize and compress images on your website to improve performance.
- **Google Analytics**: This plugin allows you to track and analyze the traffic and behavior of your website visitors.
- **Advanced Custom Fields**: This plugin allows you to add custom fields to your posts, pages and custom post types, it's useful for creating custom pages and forms.

It's important to note that not all the plugins are necessary for every website and it's always recommended to check the reviews, ratings and compatibility of the plugin before installing it. It's also important to keep in mind that having too many plugins installed can slow down your website.

CHAPTER TWELVE

How to speed up the WordPress site?

There are several ways to speed up a WordPress website:

- **Optimize images**: Large image files can slow down a website, so it's important to optimize and compress images before uploading them to your site. You can use plugins like WP Smush or ShortPixel to optimize images automatically.
- **Use a Content Delivery Network (CDN)**: A CDN allows you to distribute your website's static files (such as images, CSS and JavaScript files) across multiple servers around the world. This can help to reduce the load on your server and speed up your website for users who are located far from your server.
- **Minimize the use of plugins**: Having too many plugins installed can slow down your website, so it's important to only use the plugins that are essential for your website's functionality.
- **Use a caching plugin**: Caching plugins like W3 Total Cache or WP Super Cache can help to speed up your website by caching and minifying your pages and posts.

- **Optimize your database**: Over time, your database can become cluttered with redundant data that can slow down your website. You can use a plugin like WP-Optimize to optimize your database and remove unnecessary data.
- **Use a fast hosting**: A good web hosting provider can make a big difference in the speed of your website, make sure to use a fast and reliable hosting provider.
- **Use a good theme**: A good theme can make a big difference in the speed of your website, make sure to use a lightweight and well-coded theme.

CHAPTER THIRTEEN

Few Known Successful people in Blogging

There are many successful bloggers in various fields, but some of the most notable and successful bloggers include:

- **Pat Flynn**: Pat Flynn is the founder of the blog Smart Passive Income, which focuses on online business and internet marketing. He's a popular speaker and author and is known for his transparency and honesty in his blogging.
- **Neil Patel**: Neil Patel is the founder of Quick Sprout and Neil Patel Digital, which provides digital marketing advice and services. He's a well-known expert in SEO, analytics, and conversion optimization.
- **Brian Dean**: Brian Dean is the founder of Backlinko, a website that focuses on SEO and link building. He's a well-known expert in SEO and content marketing, and has been featured in various publications.
- **Harsh Agrawal**: Harsh Agrawal is the founder of ShoutMeLoud, a website that focuses on blogging, WordPress, and online marketing. He's a well-known expert in digital marketing and has helped thousands of people to start their own blogs and online businesses.

- **Michael Hyatt**: Michael Hyatt is the founder of MichaelHyatt.com, a website that focuses on leadership, productivity, and personal development. He's a bestselling author, speaker, and business consultant.
- **Darren Rowse**: Darren Rowse is the founder of ProBlogger, a website that focuses on blogging and online business. He's a well-known expert in blogging and has helped thousands of people to start their own blogs and make money from them.

These are just a few examples of successful bloggers, there are many other bloggers who have made a name for themselves in different niches and have been able to build a successful business out of blogging.

CHAPTER FOURTEEN

Helpful Youtube channels in Blogging?

There are many YouTube channels that provide helpful tips and advice on blogging, some popular ones include:

- **Smart Passive Income**: Pat Flynn's YouTube channel, which provides tips on how to create a successful online business and blog.
- **Neil Patel**: Neil Patel's YouTube channel, which provides tips on SEO, analytics, and digital marketing.
- **Backlinko**: Brian Dean's YouTube channel, which provides tips on SEO and link building.
- **ShoutMeLoud**: Harsh Agrawal's YouTube channel, which provides tips on blogging, WordPress, and online marketing.
- **Michael Hyatt**: Michael Hyatt's YouTube channel, which provides tips on leadership, productivity, and personal development.
- **ProBlogger**: Darren Rowse's YouTube channel, which provides tips on blogging and online business.
- **Blogging Tips**: A YouTube channel that provides tips on blogging and online business, run by a blogger named Ankit Singla.

- **Blogging Wizard**: A YouTube channel that provides tips on blogging, SEO, and content marketing, run by a blogger named Adam Connell.
- **Blogging Your Passion**: A YouTube channel that provides tips on blogging and online business, run by a blogger named Jeanette S.
- **Blogging With Fun**: A YouTube channel that provides tips on blogging, SEO, and online marketing, run by a blogger named Ruchika.

These channels offer a wealth of information on various aspects of blogging, from creating content to monetizing your blog, and can be a great resource for both new and experienced bloggers.

www.ingramcontent.com/pod-product-compliance
Lightning Source LLC
Chambersburg PA
CBHW030509170726
47990CB00008BA/3125